Copyright © 2020 Mary L George

All rights reserved. No part of this book may be reproduced or used in any manner without the prior written permission of the copyright owner, except for the use of brief quotations in a book review.

Hardcover: ISBN# 9781735364902
eBook: ISBN# 9781735364919

Edited by Kimberlina Gordon
Cover Art by Delores Janet George & Mary L George

Scripture quotations taken from the Amplified Bible (AMP), Copyright © 2015 by The Lockman Foundation. Used by permission. www.lockman.org

Scripture quotations taken from the Amplified Bible (AMPC),
Copyright © 1954, 1958, 1962, 1964, 1965, 1987 by The Lockman Foundation
Used by permission. www.lockman.org

Scripture taken from the New King James Version. Copyright © 1982 by Thomas Nelson. Used by permission. All rights reserved.

Scripture quotations from The Authorized (King James) Version. Rights in the Authorized Version in the United Kingdom are vested in the Crown. Reproduced by permission of the Crown's patentee, Cambridge University Press

The George Family Library Publishing Company
www.thegeorgefamilylibrary.com

www.thegeorgefamilylibrary.com

Dedicated To Mama

We Love You

www.thegeorgefamilylibrary.com

www.thegeorgefamilylibrary.com

It winked at me.
And then...

It wrapped its arms around me.
I shivered in its hug.

It caused me to sing,
to tap my feet,
to jump about.

How could anything be more refreshing? It was so special!

For some time we frolicked together.

We played hide-and-seek, tag, and all those other neat kid games.

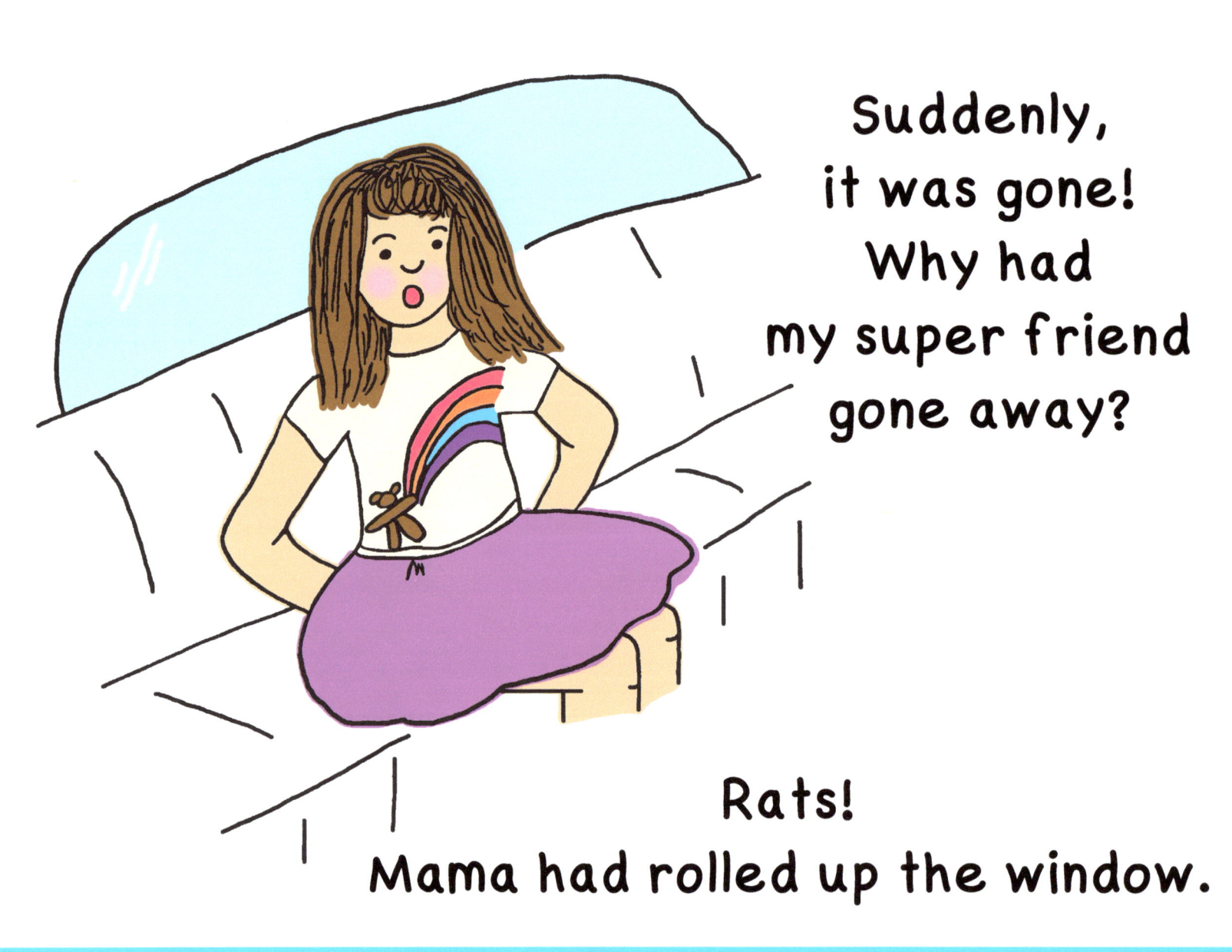

Suddenly, it was gone! Why had my super friend gone away?

Rats! Mama had rolled up the window.

My new friend was gone.
But its memory lingered on.

Yep, today I played like a friend
with the summer wind
while riding in the backseat of the car!

I'm older now. The wind still delights me.
It's movements are ever changing,
yet it is continually consistent.

The wind reminds me of the Holy Spirit.

He is moving and changing directions, yet His character is always the same.

Jude 1:25, Hebrews 13:8

I am reminded that my Savior, Yeshua – Jesus, gave His life for my life...

...and I have liberty through Him.

John 3:16-17, Titus 3:4-6, Ephesians 2:8-9, 2 Corinthians 3:17, Galatians 5:13

The Holy Spirit is now living inside me.
He is my Forever Friend through the sacrifice of blood of Yeshua Messiah - Jesus Christ.
He is moving and changing me to be more like Him….

Colossians 1:19-20, Isaiah 53:5, 1Peter 2:24, Joshua 1:9, Galatians 5:22-25, 2 Corinthians 9:6-7

FAITHFUL

GENEROUS

LOVING

Kind

STRONG

BRAVE!

Wise

discerning

Should you want the wind of the Holy Spirit inside of you as your forever friend,  put your hand over your belly where your spirit heart is, and say this prayer with me. ...

John 7:38, Romans 10:8-13

Jesus, I believe
You are my Savior.
You are fully God and fully man.
You poured your
blood on the cross for
my sins – everything that separates
me from You, such as, my disobedience.
I receive Your free gift of salvation.
I now ask You to
come inside me,
Holy Spirit, and live inside
me forever.

Move and help me each day to be
changed inside, so I can be
more and more like You.
Let me not walk away from You and
Your forever love and friendship.
Thank You for making me
Your child and friend right now.
In Jesus' beautiful name.
Amen.

As you get to know the Holy Spirit more by reading your Holy Bible,...

talking with Him, and listening to Him every day, you will recognize Him and the changes He continues to make inside you.

Romans 7:22, James 1:25, John 14:15-18, John 14:21, Exodus 20:1-23, 1 Cor. 13:1-18a

Always ask and receive His forgiveness quickly when you do something that the Holy Spirit told you not to do, so that your heart does not grow hard and not listen to your forever friend, the Holy Spirit, any more.

Psalm 95:8, Proverbs 28:14, Hebrews 3:15, Revelation 3:19, 1 Thessalonians 5:19-20, Ephesians 4:30

www.thegeorgefamilylibrary.com

Jude 1:25 (AMPC)
"To the one only God, our Savior through Jesus Christ our Lord, be glory (splendor), majesty, might and dominion, and power and authority, before all time and now and forever (unto all the ages of eternity). Amen (so be it)."

Hebrews 13:8 (AMPC)
"Jesus Christ (the Messiah) is [always] the same, yesterday, today, [yes] and forever (to the ages)."

John 3:16-17 (AMPC)
"For God so greatly loved and dearly prized the world that He [even] gave up His only begotten (unique) Son, so that whoever believes in (trusts in, clings to, relies on) Him shall not perish (come to destruction, be lost) but have eternal (everlasting) life. For God did not send the Son into the world in order to judge (to reject, to condemn, to pass sentence on) the world, but that the world might find salvation and be made safe and sound through Him."

Titus 3:4-6 (AMPC)
"But when the goodness and loving-kindness of God our Savior to man [as man] appeared, He saved us, not because of any works of righteousness that we had done, but because of His own pity and mercy, by [the] cleansing [bath] of the new birth (regeneration) and renewing of the Holy Spirit, Which He poured out [so] richly upon us through Jesus Christ our Savior."

Ephesians 2:8-9 (AMP)
"For it is by grace [God's remarkable compassion and favor drawing you to Christ] that you have been saved [actually
delivered from judgment and given eternal life] through faith. And this [salvation] is not of yourselves [not through your own effort], but it is the [undeserved, gracious] gift of God; not as a result of [your] works [nor your attempts to keep the Law], so that no one will [be able to] boast or take credit in any way [for his salvation]."

2 Corinthians 3:17 (AMPC)
"Now the Lord is the Spirit, and where the Spirit of the Lord is, there is liberty (emancipation from bondage, freedom)."

Galatians 5:13 (NKJV)
"For you, brethren, have been called to liberty; only do not use liberty as an opportunity for the flesh, but through love
serve one another"

Colossians 1:19-20 (NKJV)
"For it pleased the Father that in Him all the fullness should dwell, and by Him to reconcile all things to Himself, by Him, whether things on earth or things in heaven, having made peace through the blood of His cross."

Isaiah 53:5 (NKJV)
"But He was wounded for our transgressions, He was bruised for our iniquities;The chastisement for our peace was upon Him, and by His stripes we are healed."

1 Peter 2:24 (NKJV)
"Who Himself bore our sins in His own body on the tree, that we, having died to sins, might live for righteousness-by whose stripes you were healed."

Joshua 1:9 (NKJV)
"Have I not commanded you? Be strong and of good courage; do not be afraid, nor be dismayed, for the Lord your God is with you wherever you go."

Galatians 5:22-25 (NKJV)
"But the fruit of the Spirit is love, joy, peace, longsuffering, kindness, goodness, faithfulness, gentleness, self-control. Against such there is no law. And those who are Christ's have crucified the flesh with its passions and desires. If we live in the Spirit, let us also walk in the Spirit."

2 Corinthians 9:6-7 (AMP)
"Now [remember] this: he who sows sparingly will also reap sparingly, and he who sows generously [that blessings may come to others] will also reap generously [and be blessed]. Let each one give [thoughtfully and with purpose] just as he has decided in his heart, not grudgingly or under compulsion, for God loves a cheerful giver [and delights in the one whose heart is in his gift]."

John 7:38 (KJV)
"He that believeth on me, as the scripture hath said, out of his belly shall flow rivers of living water."

John 7:38 (NKJV)
"He who believes in Me, as the Scripture has said, out of his heart will flow rivers of living water."

John 7:38 (AMPC)
"He who believes in Me [who cleaves to and trusts in and relies on Me] as the Scripture has said, From his innermost being shall flow [continuously] springs and rivers of living water."

Romans 10:8-13 (AMPC)
"But what does it say? The Word (God's message in Christ) is near you, on your lips and in your heart; that is, the Word (the message, the basis and object) of faith which we preach, because if you acknowledge and confess with your lips that Jesus is Lord and in your heart believe (adhere to, trust in, and rely on the truth) that God raised Him from the dead, you will be saved. For with the heart a person believes (adheres to, trusts in, and relies on Christ) and so is justified (declared righteous, acceptable to God), and with the mouth he confesses (declares openly and speaks out freely his faith) and confirms [his] salvation. The Scripture says, No man who believes in Him [who adheres to, relies on, and trusts in Him] will [ever] be put to shame or be disappointed. [No one] for there is no distinction between Jew and Greek. The same Lord is Lord over all [of us] and He generously bestows His riches upon all who call upon Him [in faith]. For everyone who calls upon the name of the Lord [invoking Him as Lord] will be saved."

Romans 7:22 (NKJV)
"For I delight in the law of God according to the inward man."

James 1:25 (NKJV)
"But he who looks into the perfect law of liberty and continues in it, and is not a forgetful hearer but a doer of the work, this one will be blessed in what he does."

John 14:15-18 (AMPC)
"If you [really] love Me, you will keep (obey) My commands. And I will ask the Father, and He will give you another Comforter (Counselor, Helper, Intercessor, Advocate, Strengthener, and Standby), that He may remain with you forever- the Spirit of Truth, Whom the world cannot receive (welcome, take to its heart), because it does not see Him or know and recognize Him. But you know and recognize Him, for He lives with you [constantly] and will be in you. I will not leave you as orphans [comfortless, desolate, bereaved, forlorn, helpless]; I will come [back] to you."

John 14:21 (AMPC)
"The person who has My commands and keeps them is the one who [really] loves Me; and whoever [really] loves Me will be loved by My Father, and I [too] will love him and will show (reveal, manifest) Myself to him. [I will let Myself be clearly seen by him and make Myself real to him.]"

Exodus 20:1-23 (AMPC)

"Then God spoke all these words: I am the Lord your God, Who has brought you out of the land of Egypt, out of the house of bondage. You shall have no other gods before or besides Me. You shall not make yourself any graven image [to worship it] or any likeness of anything that is in the heavens above, or that is in the earth beneath, or that is in the water under the earth; You shall not bow down yourself to them or serve them; for I the Lord your God am a jealous God, visiting the iniquity of the fathers upon the children to the third and fourth generation of those who hate Me, but showing mercy and steadfast love to a thousand generations of those who love Me and keep My commandments. You shall not use or repeat the name of the Lord your God in vain [that is, lightly or frivolously, in false affirmations or profanely]; for the Lord will not hold him guiltless who takes His name in vain. [Earnestly] remember the Sabbath day, to keep it holy (withdrawn from common employment and dedicated to God). Six days you shall labor and do all your work, but the seventh day is a Sabbath to the Lord your God; in it you shall not do any work, you, or your son, your daughter, your manservant, your maidservant, your domestic animals, or the sojourner within your gates. For in six days the Lord made the heavens and the earth, the sea, and all that is in them, and rested the seventh day. That is why the Lord blessed the Sabbath day and hallowed it [set it apart for His purposes]. Regard (treat with honor, due obedience, and courtesy) your father and mother, that your days may be long in the land the Lord your God gives you. You shall not commit murder. You shall not commit adultery. You shall not steal. You shall not witness falsely against your neighbor. You shall not covet your neighbor's house, your neighbor's wife, or his manservant, or his maidservant, or his ox, or his donkey, or anything that is your neighbor's. Now all the people perceived the thunderings and the lightnings and the noise of the trumpet and the smoking mountain, and as [they] looked they trembled with fear and fell back and stood afar off. And they said to Moses, You speak to us and we will listen, but let not God speak to us, lest we die. And Moses said to the people, Fear not; for God has come to prove you, so that the [reverential] fear of Him may be before you, that you may not sin. And the people stood afar off, but Moses drew near to the thick darkness where God was. And the Lord said to Moses, Thus shall you say to the Israelites, You have seen for yourselves that I have talked with you from heaven. You shall not make [gods to share] with Me [My glory and your worship]; gods of silver or gods of gold you shall not make for yourselves."

1 Corinthians 13:1-8a (AMPC)
"If I [can] speak in the tongues of men and [even] of angels, but have not love (that reasoning, intentional, spiritual devotion such as is inspired by God's love for and in us), I am only a noisy gong or a clanging cymbal. And if I have prophetic powers (the gift of interpreting the divine will and purpose), and understand all the secret truths and mysteries and possess all knowledge, and if I have [sufficient] faith so that I can remove mountains, but have not love (God's love in me) I am nothing (a useless nobody). Even if I dole out all that I have [to the poor in providing] food, and if I surrender my body to be burned or in order that I may glory, but have not love (God's love in me), I gain nothing. Love endures long and is patient and kind; love never is envious nor boils over with jealousy, is not boastful or vainglorious, does not display itself haughtily. It is not conceited (arrogant and inflated with pride); it is not rude (unmannerly) and does not act unbecomingly. Love (God's love in us) does not insist on its own rights or its own way, for it is not self-seeking; it is not touchy or fretful or resentful; it takes no account of the evil done to it [it pays no attention to a suffered wrong]. It does not rejoice at injustice and unrighteousness, but rejoices when right and truth prevail. Love bears up under anything and everything that comes, is ever ready to believe the best of every person, its hopes are fadeless under all circumstances, and it endures everything [without weakening]. Love never fails [never fades out or becomes obsolete or comes to an end]."

Hebrews 13:5-6 (NKJV)
"Let your conduct be without covetousness; be content with such things as you have. For He Himself has said, 'I will never leave you nor forsake you.' So we may boldly say: 'The Lord is my helper; I will not fear. What can man do to me?'"

Deuteronomy 31:6 (NKJV)
"Be strong and of good courage, do not fear nor be afraid of them; for the Lord your God, He is the One who goes with you. He will not leave you nor forsake you."

Psalm 95:8 (NKJV)
"Do not harden your hearts, as in the rebellion as in the day of trial in the wilderness."

Proverbs 28:14 (NKJV)
"Happy is the man who is always reverent, but he who hardens his heart will fall into calamity."

Hebrews 3:15 (NKJV)
"While it is said: 'Today, if you will hear His voice, do not harden your hearts as in the rebellion.'"

Revelation 3:19 (NKJV)
"As many as I love, I rebuke and chasten. Therefore be zealous and repent."

1 Thessalonians 5:19 (NKJV)
"Do not quench the Spirit."

Ephesians 4:30 (NKJV)
"And do not grieve the Holy Spirit of God, by whom you were sealed for the day of redemption."

Ephesians 4:30 (AMPC)
"And do not grieve the Holy Spirit of God [do not offend or vex or sadden Him], by Whom you were sealed (marked, branded as God's own, secured) for the day of redemption (of final deliverance through Christ from evil and the consequences of sin)."

Proverbs 27:9 (NKJV)
"Ointment and perfume delight the heart, and the sweetness of a man's friend gives delight by hearty counsel."

John 3:5-8 (NKJV)
"Jesus answered, 'Most assuredly, I say to you, unless one is born of water and the Spirit, he cannot enter the kingdom of God. That which is born of the flesh is flesh, and that which is born of the Spirit is spirit. Do not marvel that I said to you, "You must be born again." The wind blows where it wishes, and you hear the sound of it, but cannot tell where it comes from and where it goes. So is everyone who is born of the Spirit.'"

www.thegeorgefamilylibrary.com

1946 -2019

Delores Janet (Ross) George

Delores Janet (Ross) George was a daughter, sister, friend, wife, mother, teacher, leader, writer, and most importantly, born again. She loved children, and she enjoyed reading stories to them. Delores Janet worked in Kindergarten over 12 years as a Teacher's Aid before going back to college to get her Bachelor of Science degree in Sociology, minoring in Psychology, and Full Clad Teacher's Credentials at California State University Chico (CSUChico). After holding her college and teaching degrees, Delores Janet wanted to give back to the community that she grew up in; so, she spent several years in the school district she grew up in substituting and teaching full time from Kindergarten to Adult Ed. Delores Janet spent much of her life working with children. In the time she worked in Kindergarten, she wrote and illustrated several children's books that she read to the classes she worked with. She always wanted her books published, but family and helping people took priority in her life. Today I Played With The Wind is her first children's book of many that her family has published in honor of her legacy she left behind. Delores Janet George passed away in January of 2019. She left behind her husband, Ralph, two daughters, son, son-in-law, daughter-in-law, and two grandsons.

Mary L George

Mary L George is the youngest daughter of Delores Janet (Ross) George. Mary holds a Bachelor of Arts in Business Management from Bethany University (BU), and an Associate of Science in Culinary Arts from Yuba College (YCCD). Mary enjoys her Savior, Yeshua Messiah - Jesus Christ; nature, arts, music, children, traveling, and life. With the influence of her mother reading books to her throughout her life, like her mother, Mary also desired to write and illustrate children's books since childhood. Today I played With The Wind is the first children's book that Mary has published. She is glad she has co-authored and co-illustrated this book and others with her mother.

www.ingramcontent.com/pod-product-compliance
Lightning Source LLC
LaVergne TN
LVHW070408080526
838200LV00089B/363